The ZOO in the house

The ZOO in the house

Discover the animals which live in your house

David Taylor & Mike Birkhead

Introduction

How many people live in your house? Three, four – perhaps as many as seven? And how many other creatures live with you? You might think that there is only your dog or cat, if you have one, but you would be wrong. Whether you live in the town or the country, in a house or a flat, a host of other species live out their lives, are born, find food, multiply and die, right alongside you. To many of them your home is their whole world. They never venture outside. They share its warmth and snugness with you, roam about its many different types of hunting-ground, sleep, mate and fight there. Some of them are very bad lodgers, while others are very houseproud.

In the average well-kept modern home, there is a whole zoo of creatures. In addition to thousands of mites, about 450 other creatures share the place with the people who live there. Read on and we'll have a look at some of them.

First published in Great Britain in 1987
Reprinted in paperback 1988
by Boxtree Limited

Text copyright © 1987 by David Taylor
Photographs copyright © 1987 by Mike Birkhead
and Alastair MacEwen

ISBN 1 85283 019 0

Front cover illustration by David Quinn
Edited by Graham Eyre
Designed by Grahame Dudley
Typeset by Servis Filmsetting Limited, Manchester
Printed in Italy by New Interlitho S.p.A. - Milan

for Boxtree Limited, 36 Tavistock Street,
London WC2E 7PB

Acknowledgements
Photographs on pp. 22, 24, 25, 30, 37 are reproduced by courtesy of Bruce Coleman Ltd., on p. 34 by the London School of Hygiene and Tropical Medicine (Electron Microscopy Laboratory) and p. 40 Oxford Scientific Films.

Contents

The Mouse	6
The Woodlouse	12
The Spider	16
The Bat	22
The Fungus	26
The Silverfish	30
The Clothes Moth	32
The Dust Mite	34
The Woodworm	38
The Ant	42

Abbreviations

mm	millimetre
cm	centimetre
m	metre
km	kilometre
ha	hectare
gm	gram
kg	kilogram

The Mouse

Mice are not ferocious animals, though a wild one will give a sharp bite if you pick it up, but they are important pests. They carry diseases and harm food-supplies, not only by eating them but also by damaging and soiling what they don't eat. Mice even helped to lose a war!

In 1796 the Austrians were facing defeat by Napoleon's armies. The Austrian generals did not know what to do, so they decided to use an ancient Greek and Roman way of working out a plan. They dipped a mouse's feet in some ink and place the animal on a map of the battlefield. It ran across the map leaving a splodgy path, and the generals sent their soldiers to the placed marked by the mouse. It didn't help though, for Napoleon won.

Mice were bred, protected and worshipped in ancient Greece and Rome. As you can tell from the story about the Austrian generals who copied the old practice of using a mouse to tell them what to do, they were thought to be magical creatures. Mouse-worship continued in Greece right up to the sixteenth century.

There are old country people alive who as children were given roasted, stewed or baked mice to eat, and some

The mouse that lost a war

people still believe that mouse is a good cure for coughs, sore throats, fevers, fits, whooping-cough and even bed-wetting! I've tasted cooked mouse, and it reminded me of tender chicken. In earlier times, mouse blood was believed to get rid of warts on the skin if dropped on them, and a seventeenth-century treatment for quinsy (a disease like tonsilitis) was to swallow a silk thread

The house mouse, a typical rodent

dipped in mouse-blood. There were many other such 'cures'.

There are some very strange legends about mice. One is that in the year 970 AD an army of mice ate alive a German bishop called Hatto in a tower on the river Rhine. The name of the tower is the Mausturm, German for 'Mouse Tower'. However, it hasn't really got anything to do with mice, and its name comes from an old German word like the word for mouse but really meaning 'toll'. Boats passing up and down the river had to pay a toll, a sort of tax, before they would be allowed to continue on their way. People must have forgotten what the name really meant, and thought up a story to explain what the tower had to do with mice. Of course mice would never eat a bishop! The typical mouse is a much shyer and more timid animal, which is what the Scottish poet Robert Burns meant when he called it a 'cow'ring, tim'rous beastie' in his famous poem about a mouse.

Like rats, mice are rodents, mammals with *one* pair of upper gnawing teeth. The difference between rats and mice is not just one of size, for there are small species of rat and large species of mouse. To scientists rats and mice are simply names given to various species within the animal family *Muridae*. Rats have more rows of scales on their tails than mice have. Rats have 210 or more, while mice never have more than 180.

You have probably seen the dull-coloured little *house mouse* and, of course, the pretty little mice bred as pets. These tame mice are very clean, and cheap to keep. But there are many other sorts of mouse in the world today. The *birch mice* of the Russian steppes leap rather than run, live in burrows and hibernate during the bitter winters. The *grasshopper mice* of North America share burrows with prairie dogs and are useful in controlling insects, their favourite food, and sometimes kill birds or other rodents. *Jumping mice* can be found in America, and there are some little-known varieties in the forests of China where the giant panda lives. They have grey, golden or yellow-brown fur, long hind legs and very long tails. Jumping mice have a wonderful sense of balance, owing to their enlarged middle ear. They also have very sharp hearing. America live over 60 species of *deer mice*, pretty creatures with big eyes. They come in lots of different colours, from white to brown and black, but always have white feet. In Australia, sure enough, there is a mouse with a pouch, the *marsupial mouse*. Despite its name, however, it is not really a mouse at all, but a tiny cousin of the kangaroo. Just like other marsupials, it carries its babies in its pouch.

Mice can spread disease to humans

The *spiny pocket mice* of the Mexican deserts have very rough fur. Russia has the delicate *Selevin's mouse*, which nobody knew about until it was discovered in 1939. This interesting little creature loves to feed on spiders and is very active at night. It can't stand more than a few minutes of sunshine without becoming ill! Between Alaska, in the far north of the American continent, and the southern tip of South

These are just a few of the many types of mice in the world. They are tough little creatures, spread very quickly and have adapted to all sorts of surroundings. House mice have been known to live within the walls of refrigerators, and to keep themselves warm in their chilly surroundings have grown longer fur!

In the wild, mice tend not to live very long – only a few weeks or months. Pet mice usually live much longer, and can reach ages of 3½ and sometimes even 5½ years. Mice have an in-built ability to find their way home, but they are almost certainly colour-blind and see everything in black and white.

Like most small rodents, including rats, they need to drink very little water and usually produce nearly all they need from the food they eat. Desert species such as the *spiny mouse* can survive happily without drinking at all. To store the water in their bodies as long as possible, such species produce few droppings and only a little urine, which is very thick. Some spiny mice can live solely on tiny amounts of sea-water, and even your ordinary house mouse can go for ages without drinking anything. Do remember, though, to make sure that your pet mice always have a supply of clean, fresh water, as they are less hardy than their wild cousins and need to be able to have a drink when they want it.

Wild mice eat all sorts of things. They will eat scraps of rotten food and even rabbit droppings! Mice that live out in the country live mainly on fruit, seeds and insects, and all mice like these if they can get them. Of course, the food they are most famous for liking is cheese, but really it is not one of their favourites at all. If you give too much of it to your pet mouse, it will make its urine very smelly. It just is not true

Shall I or shan't I?

A safe descent from cheese mountain

what R.R. Kirk says in his poem 'The Mice':

   The mice were not impressed by that

     great house
   Wherein you have your glory and your
     ease;
   Magnificence is wasted on a mouse;
   They judge all things by cheese.

The tail of the mouse is used for balancing and for holding on to things. Because it is not covered with fur, it also provides a way of getting rid of heat when the mouse is too hot. Mice in colder places need and have shorter tails than mice in warmer areas. This is why the tails of mice that live in southern Britain are 10–15 per cent shorter than the tails of mice living in the far north of the country.

Some tame mice 'dance' or 'waltz'. Like the white and coloured varieties you can buy in pet shops, these mice have been specially bred from types of house mice. They have something wrong with their inner ears and this affects their sense of balance, so that they reel about and seem to dance.

It has even been found that mice have some ability to survive under water. A scientist has kept mice for up to 18 hours in tanks of salt water filled with oxygen under high pressure. The mice 'breathed' the water and their lungs picked up the oxygen from the water, as well as they usually do from air. However, under normal conditions, where the water would contain much less oxygen, it is unlikely that the mice would have lasted so long without drowning. They are, after all, land mammals, and not designed to live under water. Do *not* try this experiment for yourself!

Everyone knows that the mouse can move very fast, and lots of other things about it seem to be speeded up. The heart of a mouse beats at the incredibly rapid rate of 500–700 beats a minute. The animal also breathes very quickly – about 80–230 times a minute. The female mouse can carry her babies inside her for as little as 13 days before they are born, though usually the gestation period (the time it takes for a baby to grow inside its mother) lasts for 19–21 days. This is one of the shortest gestation periods among mammals, whose babies are born fully developed, looking like small adults. There are 1–20 young mice in each litter (group of babies), and the mother has several litters each year. Mother mice feed their babies for about 3 weeks, and a mouse is fully grown when it is 6–8 weeks old.

House mice are not welcome in the house and people use cats, traps and poisons to get rid of them. But we should not forget that dormice, relatives of the house mouse who live in the countryside, are in danger because so many of the places where they live are being destroyed and because of the new methods used in farming. These delightful, harmless creatures badly need our help and support. Just because one species of mouse is a pest, we must not think that all species of mouse are as bad.

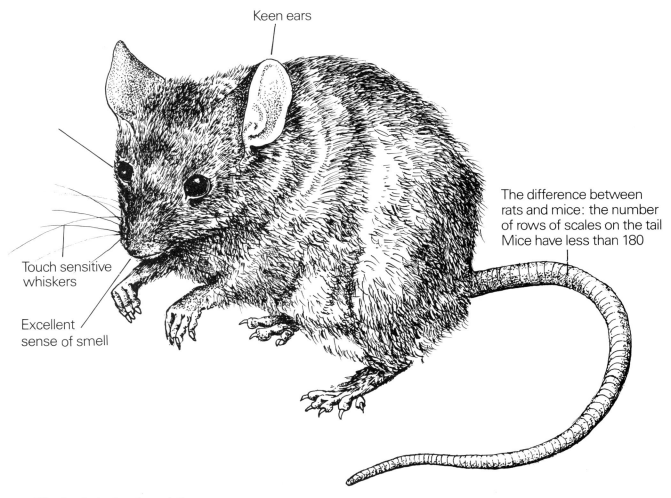

The basic body-plan of the mouse

The Woodlouse

You will often find the woodlouse about the house – in the cellar, in a pile of old timber, in the greenhouse or in the garden shed. In its armour plating the woodlouse looks like a tiny armadillo or a miniature tank. Most people know nothing about this little creature, which likes to mess about around wood.

The group of Crustaceans to which the woodlouse belongs are called *Isopods*. The Isopods are a varied group and highly successful species most of which live in water (salt water or fresh). Indeed, the woodlouse is the only Isopod that lives on land and breathes air. The other Isopods all look fairly similar to woodlice. Some are giants 35 cm long

The woodlouse is not an insect, or a relative of the armadillo (which is a mammal), but a relative of the lobster, the crab, the shrimp and the prawn. Like them, it is a member of a large family of animals with bodies that are composed of 19 segments and covered by hard outer 'crusts' (exo-skeletons). They are called *Crustaceans*.

The woodlouse: not an insect

and 12 cm broad and live deep in the ocean. Some have been found at depths of almost 10,000 m, and other 4000 m above sea-level in the South America Andes. Some swim free in the sea; others burrow in the mud of beaches and swamps. One widespread species,

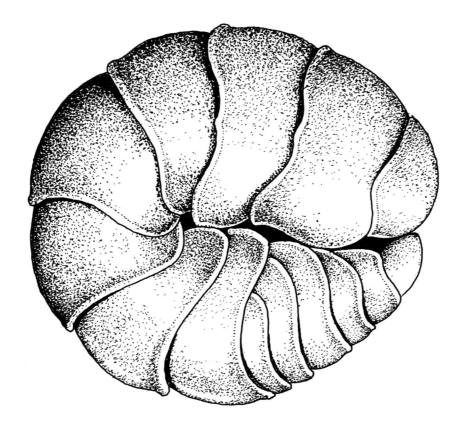

called the *gribble*, is only 3 mm long but it does a lot of damage by boring into timber under water (for instance, the wooden jetties where boats tie up, and the pilings that hold up seaside piers). Up to 70 gribbles per square centimetre have been found on badly infested timber.

Our friend the woodlouse, however, does not cause any trouble. It's a shy and nervous creature and one common British species that is found especially in areas with chalk soil has a tendency to roll up into a ball when alarmed. This is why it is called the *pill bug*.

Some years ago I tasted a favourite food of people who live in some parts of Africa – salted woodlice. They are eaten rather as we eat salted peanuts, as a handy snack. Don't turn your nose up at this! What's so odd about it when we eat the shrimps, the prawn and the crab, relatives of the woodlouse?

Hard 'crust' and 'roll up' give defence

Around 50 species of woodlouse make their homes in Britain. All have the usual armoured body-casing, but, as this is not very waterproof, they must keep out of the sun and live in damp, shady places. Otherwise most of them would dry up and die. The pill bug, however, can survive better in dry places, and you will quite often find it in warm parts of the house. Woodlice come out of their hidy-holes at night, when there is no sun to trouble them and most birds are asleep. They feed on bits of decaying plant, on soft green leaves and on moulds and other fungi. They find their food by using their antennae, which are sensitive to smell. Their insides give board and lodging to lots of friendly bacteria, which pass out with their droppings. Woodlouse-droppings look like tiny balls or pellets and you may be

The woodlouse re-cycles food

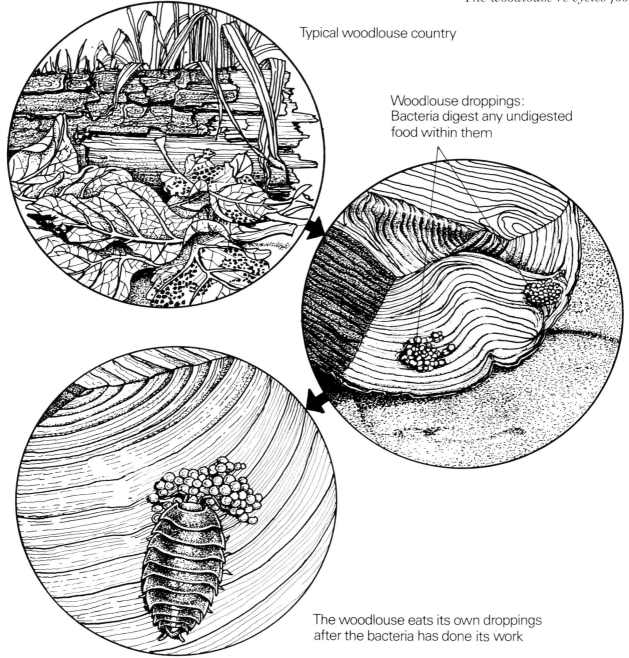

Typical woodlouse country

Woodlouse droppings: Bacteria digest any undigested food within them

The woodlouse eats its own droppings after the bacteria has done its work

able to find some under a log or stone. The bacteria digest any undigested food in the droppings and then the woodlouse eats the droppings, so that it can use the food the bacteria have digested for it. (Food that has been digested is food the body can use.) You may see your pet rabbit eating its own droppings. It does it for the same reason as the woodlouse does. This process for using food again is called 'recycling', and it is good for the soil.

The commonest species of woodlouse is (surprise, surprise!) the *common woodlouse*, which is up to 15 mm long and has a medium- to dark-grey body with pale edges to the 'armour'. Like insects and other animals that carry their skeletons on the outside of their bodies, the woodlouse has to shed its outer shell in order to be able to grow. It moults in two parts: it sheds the front half of its shell one day, and the back half perhaps up to a week later. You may be lucky enough to find a half-new, half-old woodlouse part-way through moulting.

The female woodlouse deposits her eggs into pouches of liquid on the underside of her body. After 3–5 weeks, the eggs hatch – not as grubs, but as perfect tiny woodlice. The youngsters take about 2 years to mature and may live for a further 1–2 years.

Woodlice are fascinating and harmless creatures, and in the garden or greenhouse they do a useful job by recycling plant material. So be kind to the woodlouse when you next see it in the cellar or attic – it's one of the humblest and most ancient members of the house zoo.

Common woodlice

A family party in the potting shed

The Spider

There's an old saying that goes, 'If you wish to live and thrive, let the spider run alive.' Spiders are supposed to bring good luck, and in Britain and other cooler countries are useful and harmless to man.

Spiders have been thought lucky for hundreds of years, and there is an ancient legend which says that a spider protected the infant Jesus and his parents during their flight into Egypt. Pursued by Herod's soldiers, they hid in a cave and a spider at once wove a thick web across the cave-mouth. A dove alighted on the web and laid an egg among the strands, and when the soldiers arrived at the cave and saw the web and the egg lying there, they assumed that no one could possibly have entered the cave for a long time and went on their way without looking inside.

Spiders are not insects but members of a group of animals called *Arachnids*. Like insects, these animals are arthropods (creatures that have joints in their legs), but they have no wings and have 8 legs (insects have 6). Other

The legend of Jesus and the spider

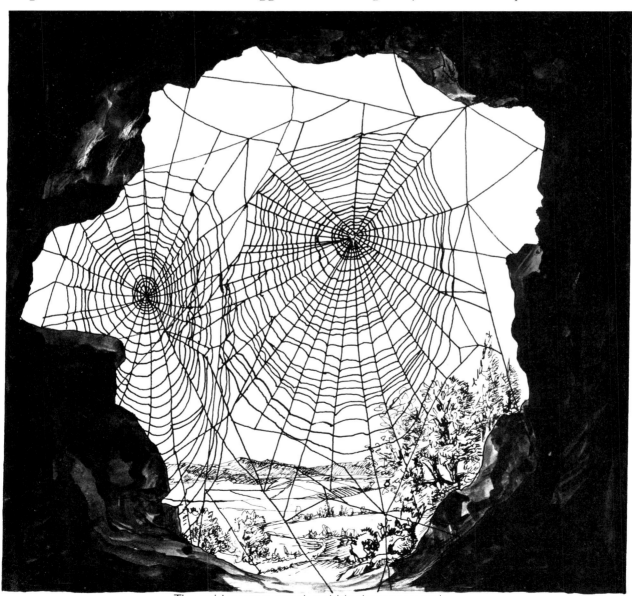

The spider wove a web to hide the cavemouth

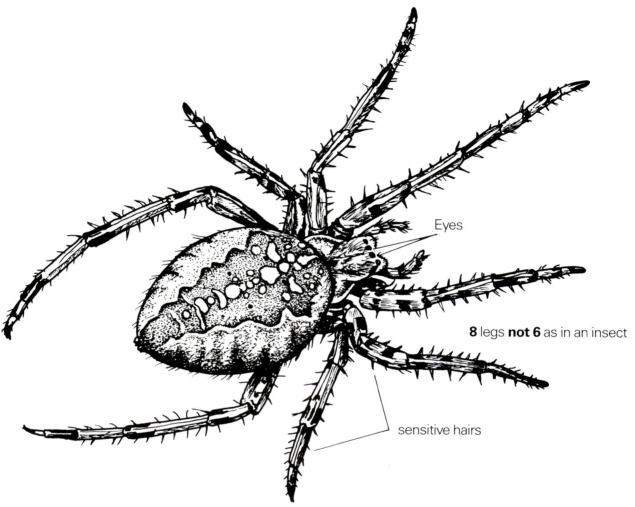

Arachnids are scorpions, ticks and mites. They breathe through a network of air-filled tubes in the body-surface and in some cases through organs called 'book lungs', which are similar to a fish's gills. Like other arthropods, such as insects and Crustaceans, Arachnids have a hard body shell or 'exo-skeleton' that has to be shed from time to time so that the creature can grow. Arachnids have no antennae, but the sensitive hairs or bristles on their body and legs act in a similar way to antennae.

The earliest known spider lived 370 million years ago. There are now approximately 40,000 species in the world, from Greenland and Alaska in the north to the southern tip of South America. Some live under water and

Body plan of typical spider

A Mexican red-knee bird-eating spider

others at up to 7300 m above sea-level. The biggest spider in the world is the famous *bird-eating spider*, which can be 25 cm across with its legs stretched out. Although it might not look it, it is not at all dangerous to man; but it still needs to be handled carefully. It can sometimes give a painful bite and the hairs on its body may cause an itchy rash on the skin.

British spiders range in size from the *six-eyed spider*, which has a body about 2 cm long, to a rare kind of *money spider* found so far only in a New Forest swamp and on a heath in Surrey. Its body is only 1 mm long. Abroad there are even smaller spiders; one kind that lives in moss in the Pacific island of Samoa is less than 0.5 mm long.

Not all spiders spin webs, but most of those you will find around the house do. The *house spider*'s web is usually quite closely meshed (with the strands quite close together) and can be 15 cm across (compare that to the webs of Australian and Indian spiders, which may be 3 m or even 5 m wide! The *daddy-long-legs spider*, which is commoner in the south of England than further north, spins a fine, very flimsy web. The *four-spotted orb spider* is red-brown in colour with four white spots, and is usually seen in the garden, and the yellow and black *spitting spider* squirts a jet of silk at its prey from a distance of up to 10 mm, binding it to a wall or a plant stem.

British spiders that do not make webs include the large *wolf spider*, which has a long black body with an orange-yellow stripe down the middle of its back.

The harmless house spider

When resting, it holds its two pairs of front legs close together. I often see this spider hunting around the pool in my back garden. The *buzzing spider* is very common in gardens and has a pale-coloured body with dark, arrow-like markings. The *zebra spider* is striped black and white, can jump up to 10 cm and is fond of walls and windows, while the *common crab spider* has a plump white or yellow body and is to be found in gardens in southern England.

The spitting spider, a spitter

The *house spider* is the species most often found in the house zoo. It is dull brown and up to 10 mm long. Often this spider turns up in the bath or sink – not because it's climbed up the drain, but because it's fallen in or come for a drink of water (there's usually a little near the plug-hole). As the sides of the bath or sink are smooth, the spider can't climb up again, because it doesn't have the sticky feet of insects such as the cockroach.

The zebra spider, a jumper

A crab spider eats a robber fly

Like all spiders, house spiders are marvellously made. They have glands that feed poison to their fangs, and after killing their prey they suck in its body-juices. House spiders and all other British spiders cannot injure humans; indeed, all the spiders that catch their prey in webs tend not to use their poison at all, except when it is the only way to defend themselves.

Spiders possess a highly developed nervous-system. The house spider can see fairly well, and the wolf spider uses the sun as a compass in a similar way to bees, but the most important of all the senses to a spider is the sense of touch. Web-building spiders send messages by 'plucking' at the strands of their webs. Males signal to females. Warning or feeding signals are sent by a mother to her young. Some male spiders attach a thread to the female's web and then use it as a sort of 'phone line, by plucking it with a certain rhythm. A spider can immediately tell what sort of creature has been caught in its web – a bee, a fly or some other insect – by the vibrations it feels. If the prey is a large and dangerous animal such as a bee, the spider may decide simply to cut it free. Spiders have a poor sense of smell, but scientists think that they can hear well.

Most fascinating is a spider's silk-making ability. On the abdomen are 'spinnerets', which are used to form silk

Nature's brilliant designer

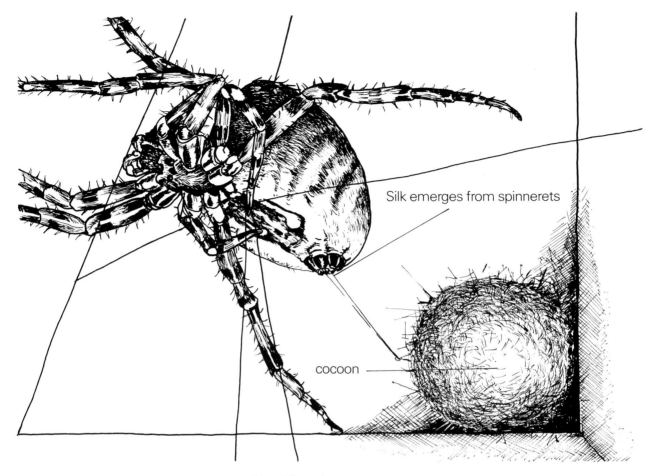

Spider silk is used in cocoons

into thread. The silk begins as a liquid made by special glands in the body, passes through the spinnerets and comes out at the tips of special hollow hairs called spinning-tubes on the end of the spinnerets. As soon as it comes out into the air the liquid silk turns into thread. Each silken thread produced by the spider is in fact a rope composed of many fine single threads each only about 0.0003 mm across. Spider silk is finer, lighter and stronger than silk-worm silk, but, unlike silkworm farms, spider-silk farms have never made much money. Most species of spider use their silk for purposes other than catching insects: they use it to make cocoons for eggs, to line their burrows, to make hinges for trap-doors, and so on. Some spiders can use up to 4000 m of thread to make just cocoon. By coating their feet with a special oil, spiders make sure they do not get caught in their own web.

Female spiders lay eggs in silken cocoons. The baby spiders or 'spiderlings' hatch from the eggs, and live on egg yolk stored in their intestines until the yolk is all used up and their digestive systems are ready for more solid food. When this happens, they go off on their own before getting hungry and starting to eat one another! As they grow they moult about 7 or 8 times, shedding the entire skin and also the cornea (the clear front part of the eye), the lining of part of the digestive system and the breathing organs. House spiders are the second longest-living British species, sometimes living for 7 years.

Never forget that spiders are useful members of the house zoo.

The Bat

As evening falls, day begins for the animal that is the most endangered of all the characters in the house zoo – the bat or 'flittermouse'. How lucky you are if your roof or a nearby church-tower has been chosen as home by this creature, the only mammal that can really fly.

In the past, people thought of the bat as an evil creature that drinks blood. It was linked with bad luck, death and witchcraft. Some people still think like this, but it's all a lot of nonsense – or nearly all, for there is one South American bat that feeds on blood. All the other bats are wonderful, harmless animals who are man's friends. Despite this, it is because of man that the number of bats in Britain and in many other countries is falling. New houses do not have places for bats to live in. The treatment of old timbers with chemicals (for woodworm and other pests) can kill bats by poisoning them. There are also fewer good hunting-grounds for bats to catch insects. All the British species of bat have suffered, but at least they are now strictly

Long-eared bat and moth

My favourite, the butterfly bat

protected by the law.

It is good to see old superstitions about bats dying away. The idea that bats can get tangled up in your hair is rubbish – the bat's sonar beam, which helps it to find a moth in total darkness and tells it when there is any obstacle in the way so that it can avoid bumping into it, means that it is hardly likely even to brush against a human head! The sonar beam is a stream of high-pitched sounds that the bat sends out. These bounce off anything in the bat's flight-path, and return as echoes to the bat's ears so that it can tell where it is. Man has learned from the bat and developed a system called radar, like the bat's sonar, that aeroplanes use so that they can fly by night.

A quarter of all species of mammal are bats: there are 951 different kinds of bat in the world today. The names of some of the species are quite delightful. Among them are *dawn bats*, *leaf-nosed bats*, *bulldog bats*, *thumbless bats*, *wrinkle-lipped bats*, *fish-eating bats*, *red bats*, *grey bats*, *brown bats*, *bamboo bats* and *painted bats*. I think my favourite is the *butterfly bat*, which has white spots and stripes in its fur and patterned wings. When it hangs in a tree, it looks just like a twist of dead leaves.

Bats feed on lots of different things, and each species tends to have one favourite food. This can be insects, scorpions, shrimps, mice, other bats, lizards, frogs, fish, fruit, flowers, pollen and even the blood of other animals. The species found in Britain eat insects, and the *horseshoe bat* loves to hunt cockchafers in the spring.

Some bats can migrate over distances as great as 2000 km. Their wings flap, so that unlike other mammals they really do fly. Creatures such as flying squirrels do not really fly at all: they simply

stretch out flaps of skin along the side of the body so that they can glide down from trees. The bat often uses its wings to catch insects, with the bit between the hind legs acting as a sort of scoop. Some bats can fly at almost 40 miles per hour.

Certain species of bat, such as *flying foxes*, can see very well, and *fruit-eating bats* have a good sense of smell. Most species rely on an incredibly highly developed sense of hearing, which allows them to fly and hunt in the dark by using their sonar beam. The ears are big, and bats' faces, which many people think are ugly, are specially designed to pick up sound. The bat's sonar bleeps, which are usually too high for humans to hear, are made through the mouth or, in some species, the nose. Some bats can continue sending out sounds while feeding, by 'whistling' through a gap in their teeth.

While some species migrate to warmer places in winter, many others hibernate

Bat faces are hardly pretty

The bat's amazing sonar system

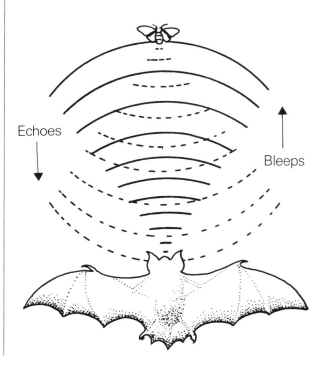

during cold weather. They select suitable hide-outs, such as caves or treeholes, where it is warm and damp. This helps them to do without water while they are asleep. When they have found the right place, they become dozy, their body temperature drops, and their breathing-rate and heart-beat slow down. This saves energy and stops the body fat from being used up too quickly. During summer and autumn, bats get ready for hibernation by building up their body fat. When they wake in spring, they may have lost one third of their body weight. During hibernation they wake up from time to time – in order to urinate! Bats can reach an age of 30 years or more.

One bat, the *vampire bat* from South America, lives by drinking the blood of domestic animals and sometimes that of human beings. Vampire bats are very fussy about which victims they attack. They prefer certain breeds of cattle and also select cows rather than bulls and calves rather than adults. The vampire bat can carry many diseases, including the terrible rabies.

The only dangerous bat: the vampire

The Fungus

Zoos need other living things besides animals. Animals need plants for food and shelter, and plants often need animals to pollinate them and destroy pests. The good zoo not only uses plants as a food source for vegetarian species, but also makes important use of trees, bushes, grass and flowers to help the animals feel at home. Humans in the zoo in the house like to have plants around them, and there must be few homes without a garden, window-box, potted plants or vases of flowers. But other plants come uninvited to make their home in the house zoo. Of these the commonest by far are the fungi, which I think the most bizarre and interesting members of the plant kingdom.

Fungi are a vast group of plants which do not possess the green chemical chlorophyll, which other plants use to make food from carbon dioxide, a gas in the air. Some fungi are the lowest known forms of plant life. They have bodies which are either simple cells or branching tubes. They reproduce by means of spores or 'seed' cells. As they cannot make their own food they have to pinch it either from dead plants or animals (fungi that do this are called 'saprophytes') or, less commonly, from living things (as 'parasites'). Some fungi can obtain food in either way. Most

A bad case of dry rot

fungi are saprophytes and they are a most important part of the never-ending cycle of death and life in nature. All sorts of waste material and dead and decaying things are food for fungi: old leaves, the remains of plants, broken branches and fallen trees, and the droppings and dead bodies of animals.

Most fungi, of which there are at least 120,000 species, live in parts of the world where it is fairly warm and damp. They are everywhere, and are one of the oldest kind of living things, although their soft and delicate tissues do not show up well in fossils.

The most familiar fungus is the edible mushroom and there are many other varieties of 'toadstool' to be found in the woods and fields, particularly in autumn, ranging from the pretty but poisonous *fly agaric* to the *black* or *white truffle*, which lives underground in beech-woods and is considered a great delicacy. Some fungi are very useful indeed to man; the yeasts that make bread rise and are used to make hops into beer and grape-juice into wine are all fungi, and so are the moulds from which penicillin and other antibiotics (used to fight all sorts of illnesses) are made. Other fungi cause disease in humans and other creatures.

But about the house the fungi you're most likely to come across are the moulds. These white, green or black furry patches can be found growing on stale food of every kind, on jam, damp clothing and leather, wallpaper and plaster. If you have a microscope, scrape some mould off an old crust of bread and magnify it as much as you can.

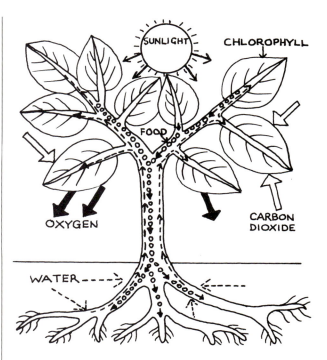

Unlike plants, the fungus does not make food

You'll easily see the network of hyphae (small branching tubes) and the darker, rounded spore-containing bodies. Where do the moulds come from? As I have said, these fungi are everywhere, and

A mouldy piece of bread

their spores, too tiny to see without a microscope, blow about in the wind and draughts and are dropped all over the place. When the spores land on something they can grow on, they absorb water and swell. The outer coat breaks open and a tube sprouts. This tube soon begins to branch and is the beginning of a new network of hyphae. The hyphae absorb liquids from the food the fungus is growing on, and help the process by passing out enzymes, which break down the food so that it can be absorbed easily.

Other very unwelcome fungi in the house zoo are the species that cause 'dry rot'. These fungi feed on timber, making it lighter, weaker and more brittle. Eventually the wood warps and cracks if the dry rot is not treated. Here again we see a fungus living on dead plant material. The hyphae of the dry-rot fungus work their way into wood, absorbing food, while on the surface the fungus may form thick layers shaped like cakes (or even mushrooms). Although the disease is called '*dry* rot', the fungi that cause it need water to be able to live, although they cannot attack wood that is too wet. 'Wet rot', on the other hand, is caused by fungi that like lots of water. Some dry-rot

Hyphae and spores of a fungus

The effect of wet-rot fungus

fungi can carry water with them over long distances, and can cause dry rot in wood that would otherwise be too dry to be affected.

Other fungi are harmless, pretty and welcome members of the house zoo. If you live in a stone house, you may be lucky enough to find lichens growing on the walls outside. Lichens are a mixture of two sorts of plant – fungus and algae (tiny blue-green plants that contain the chemical chlorophyll). The fungus provides water and salts, and the spores that allow the lichen to spread, and the algae feed the fungus with sugary food. The two need each other to survive, and the process whereby they work together is called 'symbiosis'.

Lichens demand clean air and will not grow where there is chemical pollution. They grow very, very slowly, with some species making no progress at all for up to 50 years. Even the fastest-spreading lichens don't grow more than 1 cm per year. A good place to find lichens is on the gravestones of country churchyards.

Lichens: signs of pure air

Close-up of lichens

The Silverfish

You must have seen this little creature. It's often found under the paper that lines cupboard drawers or larder shelves, beneath draining-boards and in other damp spots, and in garden sheds. The silverfish is about 15 mm long, and has a gleaming, silvery, narrow body with three little 'prongs' sticking out from the tail end. Because the silverfish likes sweet, sugary or starchy foods, it seeks flour and sugar in kitchens, breadcrumbs in larders, and glue in cardboard boxes.

The silverfish has been around for over 30 million years and is one of the most primitive types of insect still alive. It is a true insect, with a segmented body, 6 legs and 2 antennae, but it has no wings and it does not seem that the ancestors of silverfish ever had them. The first insects evolved from worm-like animals that were beginning to grow legs. A remarkable creature called the *Peripatus* shows us how the change probably happened and has some of the features of the worm and some of the features of the arthropods – animals, such as insects, with joints in their legs so that they can bend them. After this

A silverfish, not a fish

early stage, it seems, most insects began to grow wings, but not all of them did. Silverfish are such insects – reminders of an ancient time in the evolution of insects.

The 'silverfish' is so called because of

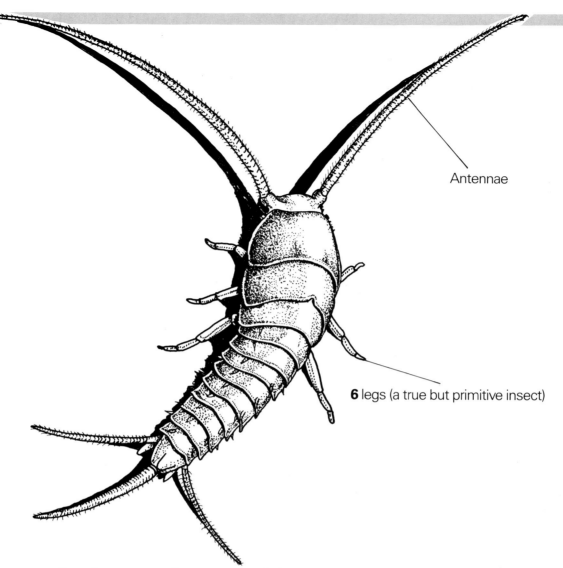

The body plan of the silverfish

the silvery scales that cover the abdomen, and the 'prongs' at the tail end, which look something like a fish's tail. Silverfish do not like dry rooms or light. They will eat almost any form of animal or vegetable matter, and if you want to keep some to study them you can easily do so by putting them in a closed jam-jar with some bits of damp blotting-paper or paper towel and breadcrumbs. They are generally no trouble and don't multiply very rapidly, but if there are lots of them they may sometimes make a nuisance of themselves by attacking starched linen or the dried glue in a book binding.

The female silverfish lays only about 20 eggs during her lifetime. They are placed in cracks and holes and are left to look after themselves. From the eggs the youngsters emerge not as grubs but as perfectly formed tiny silverfish. They take 6 months to reach their adult size, and like all insects grow by shedding their outer casings from time to time.

Silverfish have many close relatives living near the house. One likes to be out of doors and is often seen on rocks on hot days. Another, the *ant silverfish* may be found in the house and in ants' nests. Some silverfish, called *spring-tails*, have a sort of sprung tail folded beneath their abdomen. By using this tail they can jump rather like fleas. Spring-tails can often be found in gardens, flower-pots and damp cellars. Two species of true silverfish can be found throughout the year in Britain.

The Clothes Moth

The adult clothes moth has a body 1 cm long and brown or silvery-grey wings fringed at the edges, but despite its name it *doesn't* eat clothes. When it becomes an adult moth it has already chewed all the holes in woollen sweaters that it is ever going to chew, for it is the moth's larva, its caterpillar, that does all the chewing!

Clothes moths are true moths, and members of the great insect family *Lepidoptera*, which includes both butterflies and moths. They are secretive creatures and prefer to shuffle along on their legs rather than fly. The male is more active than the female and is the one usually to be seen flying. These insects existed long before man began making woollen clothes for himself and originally made their homes in birds' nests and similar places, feeding on feathers and fur. They can still be found there and around owl droppings, another source of fur and feather scraps. Clothes-moth caterpillars do not attack cotton or any man-made material.

There are two different kinds of clothes moth. The caterpillars of both sorts spin silk to form a sort of mobile home while they munch their way through life, moulting from time to time and eventually hardening into a pupa from which the adult moth emerges. The

Moths on my old sweater

caterpillars of the *case-making clothes moth* make tubes of silk and fibre within which they live and which they carry about with them. *Webbing clothes moth* caterpillars make loose silken webs as tiny protective tents over themselves where they feed.

The old-fashioned way of keeping

clothes moths away from clothes was to place 'moth balls' containing a strong-smelling substance called naptha in drawers containing clothes. Nowadays various sprays and strips that give off a vapour are used. These kill both the adult moth and the caterpillar, and are very much better than moth balls at protecting woollens and furs from attack.

The clothes moth is one of the commonest insects that attack clothes and stores in the home. There are also many others that join the zoo in the house from time to time. The larvae of the *fur beetle* eat fur, wool and flour. The *carpet beetle* has furry larvae known as 'woolly bears' that chomp the fibres of rugs and carpets. The larvae of the *larder* or *bacon beetle* stuff themselves on dried meat and animal skin, while the shiny brown larvae of the *mealworm beetle* love cereals. The grubs of the *black weevil* go for carrot leaves in the vegetable rack. Even though they may sometimes be a nuisance, none of these insects carries disease.

A clothes-moth caterpillar's tube

Clothes-moth caterpillars

The Dust Mite

Every zoo includes a number of species that can be seen in large numbers, often with their young. In the big public zoos, for instance, you can often see large groups of rhesus monkeys, lions, gazelles and some kinds of bird. So what about in the zoo in the house? Several of the creatures we are looking at in this book may well outnumber the humans in the house, even when you have visitors. But there is one kind of animal that makes its home in the house in numbers running into tens or even hundreds of thousands. This creature is the mite, a tiny relative of the spider.

The Gospel of St Mark in the Bible mentions a poor widow who threw two mites into the collection-box at the temple. The mites in that case weren't a pair of creepy-crawlies that the widow kept in a jam-jar, but the very smallest coins. The mites that live in your house are the very smallest arthropods (creatures with joints in their legs), and some are too small to be seen without a microscope. Like the spider, they have 8 legs and belong to the group of arthropods called Arachnids. There are many species of them, and they can be found all over the world, even in the frozen regions of the Arctic and Antarctic, where few creatures can survive. Some live on land, some in fresh water and some in the sea. Some of them live as parasites on animals or plants for either the whole or just part of their lives (parasites are creatures that live off other living things without doing them any good). The largest

A monster? No – a dust mite

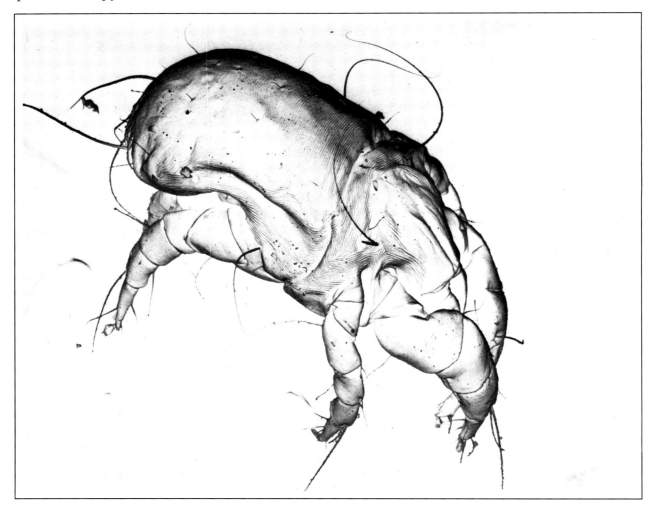

species of mite are found in the tropics. These mites can be up to 1.3 cm long and are covered with crimson velvety hairs. The bright colour warns other creatures that they are nasty to eat. One sort of mite spins webs and is sometimes called the 'money spider'. With a good magnifying glass or a microscope you may find in a drop of pond water the round red or green freshwater mites. They have long hairs on their legs to help them swim. When you are down on the beach, look for the seawater mites that creep about on seaweed.

In the garden soil or in leaf-mould under trees (especially in pine forests) there are thousands to the square metre. The mites that live closest to the surface have darker-coloured and firmer bodies than those that live deeper in the ground. Some of these mites eat rotten wood, while some prefer fungi.

The widow's mites were small coins

Parasitic mites cause a skin disease called 'mange' by feeding upon the skin scales and sucking the blood of animals; one of the commonest, which you can see without a microscope, makes its home in the ears of the domestic cat. Mites that attack plants produce a sort of 'mange' on buds, stems or leaves, often doing a lot of damage to fruit-trees. One species is responsible for the galls or swelling often found on blackcurrant bushes during May and June. The conspicuous red galls found on sycomore and maple leaves during the late summer, with up to 1000 galls on each leaf, are produced by mites. So are the pale green galls that can be seen on the leaves of blackthorn bushes throughout the summer months.

You can be sure that there are

thousands of mites going about their business in your house. *Cheese mites* may be in the larder inspecting the cheese rind. *Book mites* spend their days between the leaves of old books feeding on bits of paper and dried glue. *Grain mites* are often found feeding on cereals in the kitchen, and in grain-stores from time to time attack man, nibbling at his skin with their tough mouth-parts to cause a type of rash known as 'grocer's itch'. But the commonest creature in your household zoo is likely to be viewed in the *dust*! No house can ever be free of dust – it is a rich grey mixture of material fibres, hairs, bits of soil, wood and a thousand other substances, and skin-scales of the sort that are continuously shed throughout life by man and other animals. House-proud mothers hate dust and are always trying to get rid of it. To dust mites, however, it is a snug, dry forest. Because they too are too tiny to be seen without a microscope, dust-mites have only one major enemy, which is not an animal at all but the vacuum cleaner!

Take a pinch of dust, put it on a microscope slide, drop on a little paraffin or cooking oil, place a coverslip on top and look through the lens. With a little searching you should have no difficulty in spotting a mite among the tangle of fibres, flakes and other bits and pieces. The dust mite has a rounded, unsegmented, bag-like body with four pairs of not very long legs, pointed at the end. It has a mouth with feeding-

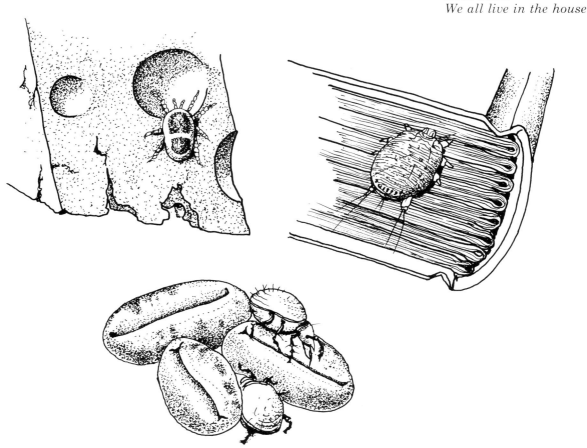

Cheese mites
Grain mites
Book mites
We all live in the house

parts that look like pincers, and segmented feelers. It breathes by means of air-tubes in the skin, like some other Arachnids and insects. There are male and female dust mites. The females lay eggs that hatch into 6 legged larvae. These then pass through a further 3 stages before becoming 8-legged adults. Some mites can reproduce from eggs that have not been fertilized by a male.

Although mites that are not parasitic do not tend to cause much harm to man, it has been found that some people are allergic to dust mites. If there is a lot of dust in the air, then when they breathe in the dust – and the dust mites – they find it very difficult to breathe. The symptoms are rather like those of the disease called asthma.

When you are next asked to do some dusting around the house, don't complain about it, but think of it as a useful way of keeping the zoo in the house from becoming overcrowded!

A scorpion, the mite's cousin

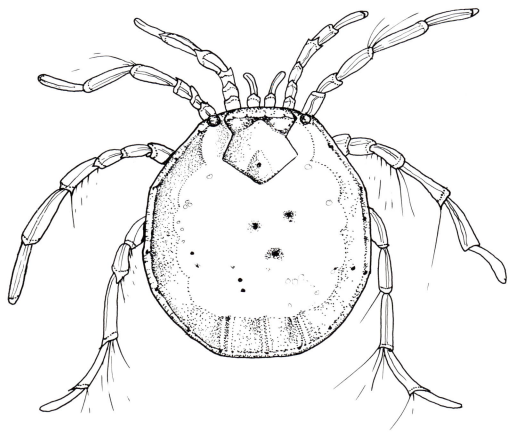

A mite's body-plan

The Woodworm

When is a worm not a worm? Answer: when it is a beetle!

I expect that on old timber beams, door-posts and antique furniture you have seen the small holes that are the entrance to tunnels bored by woodworms. However, although these holes are often seen, the creature that makes them is seen much less often. The culprit is in fact not a worm at all but the larva of a beetle.

Outside the house, many species of beetle larvae specialize in drilling tunnels in wood, eating the plant material and drinking the sap as they go. Some bore only in wood of living trees; some prefer dying or dead timber; and some like their wood to be rotting. In Britain, for example, the bright-green *musk beetle* is sometimes found on willows, where its larvae like to do their mining, and in the jungles of South America big *longhorn timber beetles*, which can be up to 20 cm long, produce huge larvae that bore into and feed upon balsa wood. These larvae are dug out by the local Indians, who think them very tasty and eat them raw or roasted. Another interesting beetle is the ambrosia beetle. Its larvae drill tunnels and chambers in wood, and the adults plant fungus gardens in these to provide food for their larvae. It is this special food that gives the beetle its name: 'ambrosia' is the food of the gods in Greek mythology and here means a rare and tasty dish! (There are also ambrosia ants, who grow gardens of

The damage to timber is caused by the larvae of the woodworm beetle

fungi in their underground nests to provide dinners for themselves and their young.) Ambrosia beetles grow their fungi on beds of wood-shavings, which are manured by the insects' droppings! One type of ambrosia beetle has the nickname 'tippling Tommy' because of its habit of drilling holes in wine or rum barrels! (A tippler is someone who drinks a lot of alcohol.)

Out of doors the larva of the *woodworm beetle* attacks deciduous trees (trees that shed their leaves in autumn), but indoors it is the commonest and most destructive insect pest that attacks woodwork. It attacks soft woods over 20 years old and hard woods more than 60 years old. Other insects that are sometimes up to the same mischief indoors are the *death-watch beetle*, which favours old oak, and the *powder-post beetle*, whose larvae go for soft wood with the sap still in it and push out dust powder behind them as they drill their holes. (The woodworm

A woodworm beetle

The larva in his tunnel: on the increase in your home

beetle's larvae push out small pellets of wood dust.) *Lymexylon* is a beetle whose larvae prefer to burrow in very hard wood.

Three quarters of all British homes are being attacked by the larvae of the woodworm beetle at this very moment!

will eventually turn the beam or chair into a crumbling shell and a pile of powder. One piece of furniture containing woodworm can infect every other piece in the same room within 6 months, so it is important to act fast if woodworms are discovered in your

The British population of this species has been steadily increasing since 1945. The adult beetle can fly and has a narrow black body. It lays its eggs in cracks on the surface of timber, and once the larvae have hatched they drill tunnels through the wood, feeding as they go. If they are not stopped, they

The death-watch beetle, often found in old churches. Its ancestors arrived with the timber from which churches were built

home!

Death-watch beetles are more commonly found in old churches, where there is often a lot of ancient oak. The beetle came into the building when the timber was originally put in place, and, if there are still beetles at work there, it is likely that they are descendants of the original beetles rather than new arrivals. Such beetle populations may therefore go back hundreds of years. They have seen bishops and priests come and go, and have steadily munched on through countless christenings, weddings and funerals.

The name 'death-watch' refers to the ticking noise made by the beetles, particularly at night. They make this noise by banging their heads on the floors of their tunnels! The banging is a sort of mating-call. The beetles can't hear, but pick up the vibrations through their highly developed sense of touch. In the past the sound of the death-watch beetle was thought to mean there was soon going to be a death in the house. In tropical countries, the larvae of some wood-eating beetles are so noisy when they eat that the sound of their gnawing deep in a tree-trunk can be heard from several metres away.

Just as public zoos and safari parks often have problems with uninvited lodgers such as pigeons, sparrows and rodents, the zoo in the house can well do without the woodworm beetle and its tunnelling relatives.

Body plan of a woodworm beetle

The Ant

The writer of the Book of Proverbs in the Bible was right when he said, 'Go to the ant, thou sluggard, consider her ways, and be wise'. (A sluggard is a lazy person.) We shall do just that, for one of the truly exotic animals in the modern zoo in the house is *pharaoh's ant* – a tropical ant that was imported by accident and is now common throughout Britain, though it can survive the cooler climate only inside heated buildings, particularly in towns. 'Pharaoh' was the title of the kings of ancient Egypt, and pharaoh's ant seems to get its name from the pharaoh in the Bible story about the plagues of Egypt (though the story says nothing about ants!)

Ants are social insects who live in well-ordered communities. They have an abdomen attached to the front part of the body by a narrow stalk, and antennae that have an 'elbow bend' in them. Sometimes they have strings on the tip of the abdomen. Ants are one of the most widespread groups of insects, and are common in nearly all parts of the world. Each colony of ants consists

Male ant

Female ant

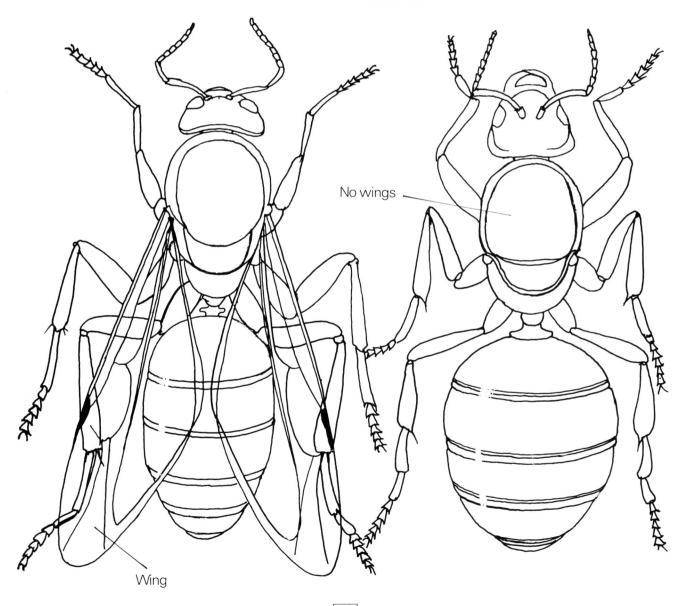

Wing

No wings

of a queen (or several queens) and a large number of workers. The workers (females who cannot lay eggs) are usually very much smaller than the queens (females who can), and are entirely wingless. The males are winged and appear only at the time of swarming, when they fertilize the queens and quickly die. The females are at first winged, but lose the wings shortly after swarming and before they raise their first brood of young. Each ant species is thus composed of females, males and workers. The more primitive ants are carnivores who hunt prey, while the more specialized and abundant types are mainly or entirely vegetarian, some even growing fungi in their nests as food for themselves and their brood.

Many ants nest in the ground, while others live in hollow twigs or burrow into wood. Some build nests of 'cardboard' made from chewed wood and saliva, and some tropical ants construct nests of leaves spun together with silk. Some ants have a powerful sting and some can't sting at all. Some ants in the tropics spend most of their time on the march and only settle down to raise their brood. These kinds are highly predatory, often travelling in great armies and destroying every living thing in their way.

The queen lays her eggs in the nest, and the workers take great care of

Anatomy of an ant's nest

Ants 'milking' aphids

them. If the colony is threatened, they take them somewhere safer. The larvae that hatch from the eggs are legless, helpless grubs that have to be fed by the workers. Their bodies are often provided with hooked bristles, and these serve as handles that the workers can use to move them about, either singly or in bundles. When fully grown, the larvae change into pupae, from which the adult ants emerge.

Around 50 species of ant live in Great Britain. The *black garden ant* is the only native British ant and is often to be found inside the house, although it does not live there. The *wood ant* builds mounds and constructs its nests inside. A single nest can contain up to a third

Red ants with their eggs

of a million workers. The *blood-red ant*, which is found only in small areas of south-eastern England and north-eastern Scotland, makes slaves of other ants. The *jet-black ant* is found mainly in the south and 'milks' aphids of the sweet honeydew that they secrete. The *Argentine ant* is a tiny thin, black ant only 2 mm long. It came to Britain from the tropics and, like pharaoh's ant, can

A seething colony of ants

only survive in heated buildings.

Pharaoh's ant is about the same size as the Argentine ant, but yellow or reddish in colour. It can now be found in almost all parts of the world. It makes its nest in the walls or beneath the floors of heated buildings. Though only 2–2.5 mm long, these little ants will often gang up to fight and drive off or actually kill and eat insects much bigger than themselves. They prefer to feed on sweet foods and some kinds of cooked meat, making long trails between their nests and the goodies they have found. Although generally regarded as a pest, pharaoh's ant can be useful. It feeds on some household pests, such as that unpleasant creature the bed bug.

Like other ants, pharaoh's ant is amazingly talented. It can learn and remember things, and can do amazing calculations when using the sun as a compass to find its way. Pharaoh's ants can see and recognize one another from a distance of around 2 cm and, like the wasp, can tell where the sun is even when it is hidden by cloud. This is because they are sensitive to light that humans cannot see.

Ants have a language of smells that they use to communicate with each other. At least 10 different scent 'words' used by ants have been deciphered by scientists. The ants leave a trail of scent shaped marks rather than an unbroken line, which would be wasteful of the precious liquid. Scent pathways laid by ant 'scouts' show the way for the marauding armies of *driver* and *army*

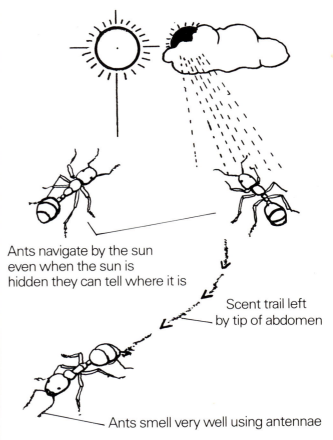

An ant's senses: they navigate by the sun and 'smell' very well

ants that sometimes march across Africa and South America.

Ants also produce special alarm smells and there are even smells released by dead ants which stimulate their living companions to hold a sort of funeral service, carrying out the body and burying it in an ant 'cemetery'. It seems that by mixing scents and varying their strengths and the pattern of their scent trails ants can communicate a whole series of different messages. Some ants also use sound, by knocking their heads on stones, cracking their mouth-parts together or using a groove on their bellies to make a strumming noise.

Pharoah's ant on jam pudding

by pushing the sting out of their abdomen and using it to squeeze a scent gland. A fine trickle of liquid is deposited, like ink running from a nib of a pen. The trail left is a series of arrow-